SIP SIP HOORAY

a bachelorette party
memory book

life

was meant for

good
friends

and

great
adventures

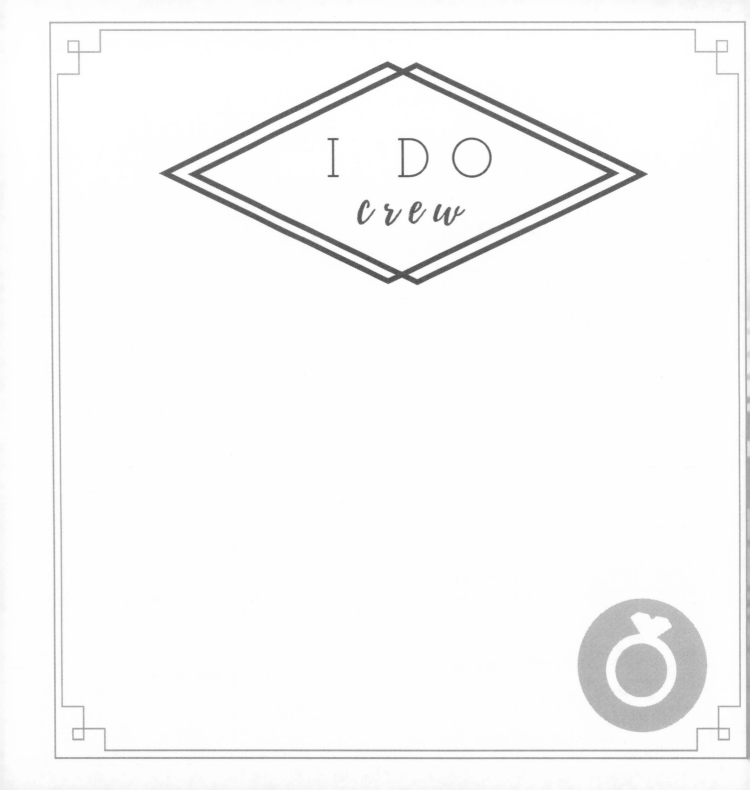

the details

The Bride To Be: _____

Maid of Honor: _____

Bridesmaids: _____

_____

_____

Location: _____

Date of Party: _____

Date of Wedding: _____

BEFORE

the party...

AFTER

the party...

kiss the miss

Leave a kiss for the miss and sign your name.

goodbye

so we don't
forget...

♪

Favorite songs: _____

_____

_____

Favorite drinks: _____

_____

_____

Favorite quotes: _____

_____

_____

memories

memories

memories

memories

a

little

party

never hurt

nobody

memories

memories

memories

memories

these are
the DAYS to
REMEMBER

memories

memories

memories

memories

memories

Made in the USA
Middletown, DE
23 March 2022